How did you do that?

Tamara has done such a good job showing tips & techniques for using Rule-It-Up's.

If it ain't broke, don't fix it! Please refer to Rule-It-Up and Rule-It-Up again.

I wanted to show you samples of pages done in full size. You can take the templates & lay them on top of the samples to see how we got there. I did a lot of cutting of paper. When you think of Round-It-Up's think big.........Trace the outside of the template with a pencil and then cut it out with the scissors. It's like super size die cuts. Tamara does a lot of things with her natural cut knife. She traces the Round-It-Up's on a full size sheet of paper. She then cut the design just enough to slip other papers inside. Lindsay made the "Title Pages" using the outside of the Round-It-Up's, then using the icons to decorate the inside. What a great way to save money. Making your own titles. I am going to tell you the items you need to do each page. Have fun, be creative and don't limit yourself.

THIS BOOK BELONGS TO...

≠ Table O' Contents ≠

Supplies

As you know the quality of the job you do depends upon the tools you use. We recommend these tools:

Templates: Of course the best quality and the cutest designs are those created by Cut-It-Up. Round-It-Up, Rule-It-Up, Trace-It-Up and Dress-It-Up.

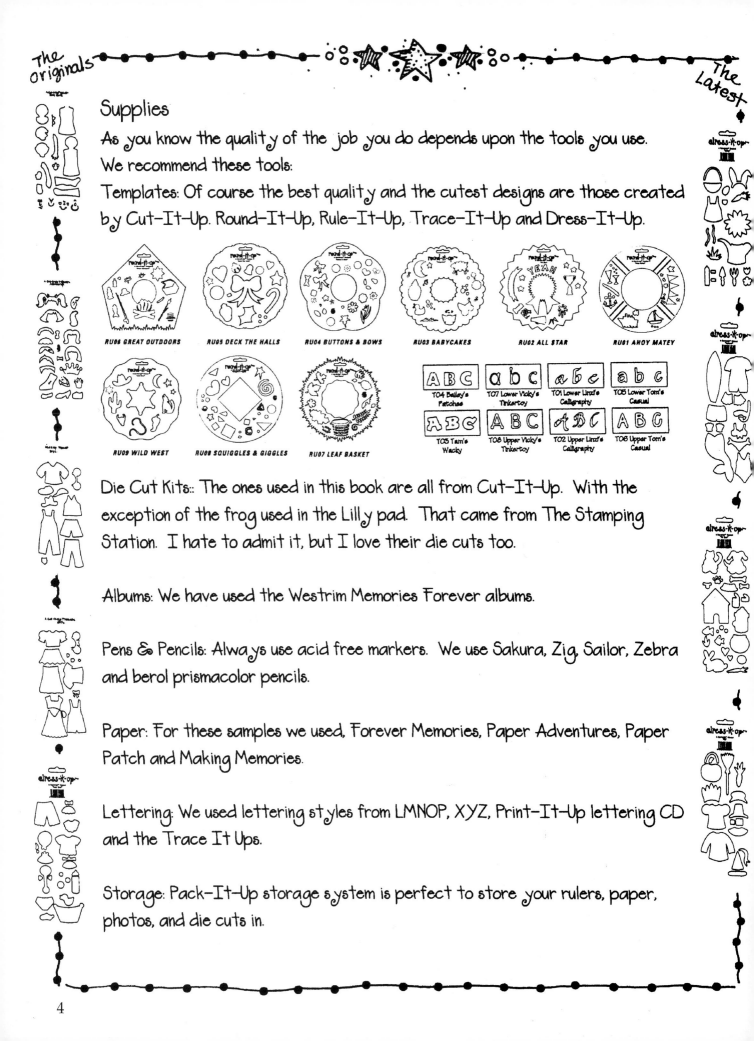

RU06 GREAT OUTDOORS   RU05 DECK THE HALLS   RU04 BUTTONS & BOWS   RU03 BABYCAKES   RU02 ALL STAR   RU01 AHOY MATEY

RU09 WILD WEST   RU08 SQUIGGLES & GIGGLES   RU07 LEAF BASKET

TO4 Bailey's Patches   TO7 Lower Vicky's Tinkertoy   TO1 Lower Linzi's Calligraphy   TO3 Lower Tom's Casual

TO3 Tam's Wacky   TO8 Upper Vicky's Tinkertoy   TO2 Upper Linzi's Calligraphy   TO6 Upper Tom's Casual

Die Cut Kits:: The ones used in this book are all from Cut-It-Up. With the exception of the frog used in the Lilly pad. That came from The Stamping Station. I hate to admit it, but I love their die cuts too.

Albums: We have used the Westrim Memories Forever albums.

Pens & Pencils: Always use acid free markers. We use Sakura, Zig, Sailor, Zebra and berol prismacolor pencils.

Paper: For these samples we used, Forever Memories, Paper Adventures, Paper Patch and Making Memories.

Lettering: We used lettering styles from LMNOP, XYZ, Print-It-Up lettering CD and the Trace It Ups.

Storage: Pack-It-Up storage system is perfect to store your rulers, paper, photos, and die cuts in.

packaging and the only photographer handy was my husband...who gladly took about 36 pictures of us. Only 1 or 2 even looked close to good. Thank you honey, good work. we needed a photo to give to West rim for some

Friends: Fall, Round-It-Up and Rule-It-Up, pens and paper and scissors. Using the center of the template, trace the photo and cut it out to put in the middle. The acorns used for the lettering are from the Fall Rule-It-Up ruler.

Sugar Pine: Camping Block-It-Ups, Fall & Great Outdoors Round-It-Up, pens, paper and scissors. Trace the outside of the Great Outdoors, cut it out, make a cut up the center and fold the flap back. Use the icons to decorate.

Main Street Warehouse: Wild West Round-It-Up, 123's of Creative Doodling. Renaissance Ribbon, pens, paper and Memories Forever decorative scissors. Trace the outside of the Wild West. Move it down and move it to the right. Fill in the middle with your colored markers. Punch two holes in the bottom and add the ribbon. Do the schwoopies and flowers around the inside of the wreath. Cut the wreath out using the decorative scissors to give it a rustic look. Adhere it to another piece of paper.

mother's
day
gardening
party
·2000·

all i wanted for
mother's day was to
plant some plants...
thanks family!

Mother's Day: Fall Found-It-Up, paper, natural cut knife. Here's an example of using the Round-It-Up to make a "pocket." Trace the Fall grass on the corner of your page. Cut out the grass leaving about one inch on each side.
Make a strip of Spring Leaves. Cut out the strip and slip it into the pocket.

willow
rose
and
carly
michelle

Sunflower Girls: All Star and Ahoy Matey Round-It-Ups. Memories Forever punch, pens, paper and scissors. Trace the outside of the All Star template. Cut it out of sunny yellow paper. Using Ahoy Matey cut the center of the sunflower. Add the punches to the outside of the circle. Finish up the detail with your pens.

My Sunflower Girls

Tom at The Nut Tree
❖1994❖
the last year it was open

Tom at the Nut Tree. Fall Round-It-Up, scissors, pen and papers. Trace the leaves on colored card stock and cut them out. Mount them on to Scrappin' Basics squares.

GOT MILK?

it's
girl
scout
cookie
time.

Got Milk? Squiggles and Giggles and Baby Cakes Round-It-Ups, scissors, pens and paper. Trace the outside of the template onto tan paper. Cut it out, then take the outside of the Baby Cakes ruler and trace the corner of the circle. Cut it out with scissors, it looks like a bite out of the cookie. Use the circles to make the chocolate chips. Adhere it to the side of the page. Fold the circle over to fit the corners.

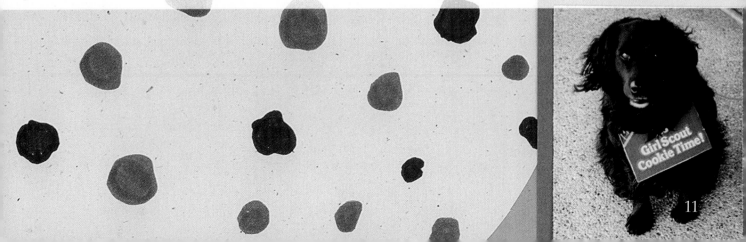

Soccer: All Star Round-It-Up, Pop-It-Up die cut template, Me & My Big Ideas stickers, scissors, paper and pens. Trace the outside of the template onto colored card stock. Cut it out and mount it on the pop-it-up template. It is adhered down in the front with Me & My Big Ideas stickers. Add the finishing touches by tracing the icons all around the page.

WALDORF

TUG O' WAR

1st

sack races & tug o' war

sacramento waldorf school

carly

the winner... carly

Tug O' War: All Star Round-It-Up Template. Tam's Wacky Trace-It-Up. Natural Cut knife, pens and paper. Trace the outside of the All Star onto the corners. Fill in with icons. Use the Tam's Wacky to do the lettering.

House Boatin': Ahoy Matey Round-It-Up, scissors, pen and paper. Trace the outside of the template onto colored card stock. Add a sailboat, then cut it out. Glue the sides and bottom on another colored card stock. Now you have a pocket.

Ashley & Carly: All Star Round-It-Up, pens and paper. Trace the outside of the template.
Leave an opening for the award seal. Color it in and add all the other icons.

Ashley & Carly

Engelbreit Lake

1st

•1990•

Faire Maiden: All Star Round-It-Up, Spring Leaves and Flowers die cut kits, scissors, pens and paper. Trace the template onto colored card stock. Cut it out and adhere it onto another piece of card stock. Stick the leaves under the wreath shape. Add flower die cuts to the top.

at the renaissance faire

Tahlia & Ariella: Bottom and Bows Round-It-Up, pens and paper. Trace the outside of the template. Move it to the right and trace again. Add the flowers and leaves. Color it in and add a few dots.

berry
special

Berry Special: Deck the Halls Round-It-Up, pens and paper. Believe it or not the berries are done with the light bulb. When you trace it, just leave the top off.

OUT FOR A NIGHT ON THE TOWN ··· LAS VEGAS STYLE!

OUT AND ABOUT, A NIGHT IN YBOR!

Movie Night: Squiggles & Giggles Round-Up, Punch-It-Up, Memories Forever punches, pens and paper.
Trace the top of the template onto black card stock. Trace the little squares and color them in with a white pen. Following the instructions in the punch book, punch the letters out using Memories Forever punches.

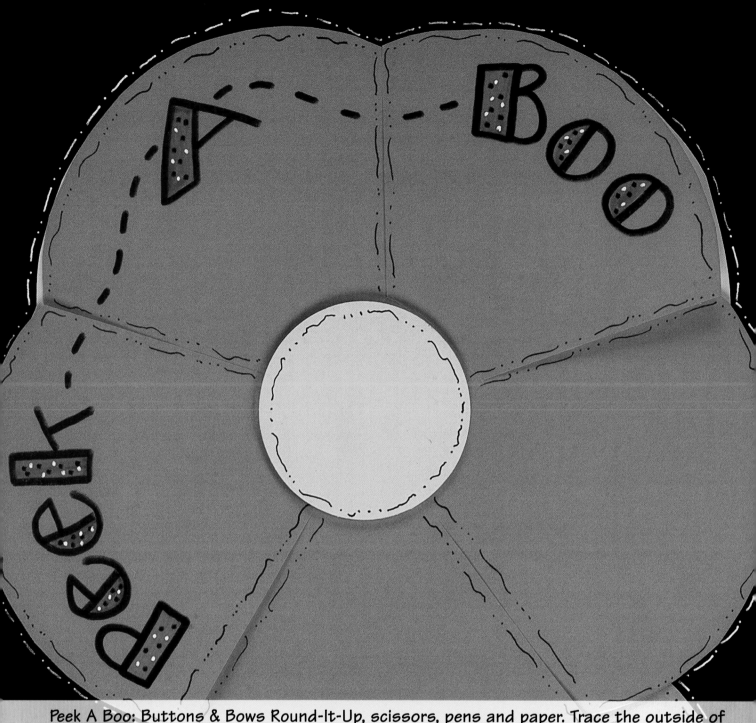

Peek A Boo: Buttons & Bows Round-It-Up, scissors, pens and paper. Trace the outside of the template onto colored card stock. Trace the inside onto a piece of yellow card stock. Cut them both out. Put the circle in the middle and cut down the strip. Put a picture underneath. Cut out leaves and tuck them under the flower.

Buttons: Buttons & Bows Round-It-Up, paper, pens, scissors, buttons die cuts, embroidery floss and buttons. Trace the outside of the template onto colored card stock. Cut it out and adhere it to the paper. Adhere the buttoms. add embroidery floss to the die cuts. Draw the buttons on the top and bottom of the page.

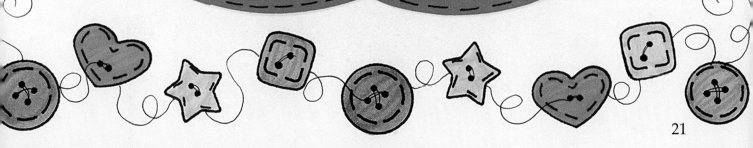

Miss New Mexico

Carly at around sixteen years

Spicy: Wild West and Ahoy Matey Round-It-Up, pens and paper. Trace the outside of the template. Add chili peppers to the bottom corner. Using Ahoy Matey draw tiny circles on the outside. Connect them to drawn lines. Cut out the center of the Ahoy Matey. Use it as a matte for your photo. Trace the circle onto your picture and cut that out to put into the center.

SPICY!

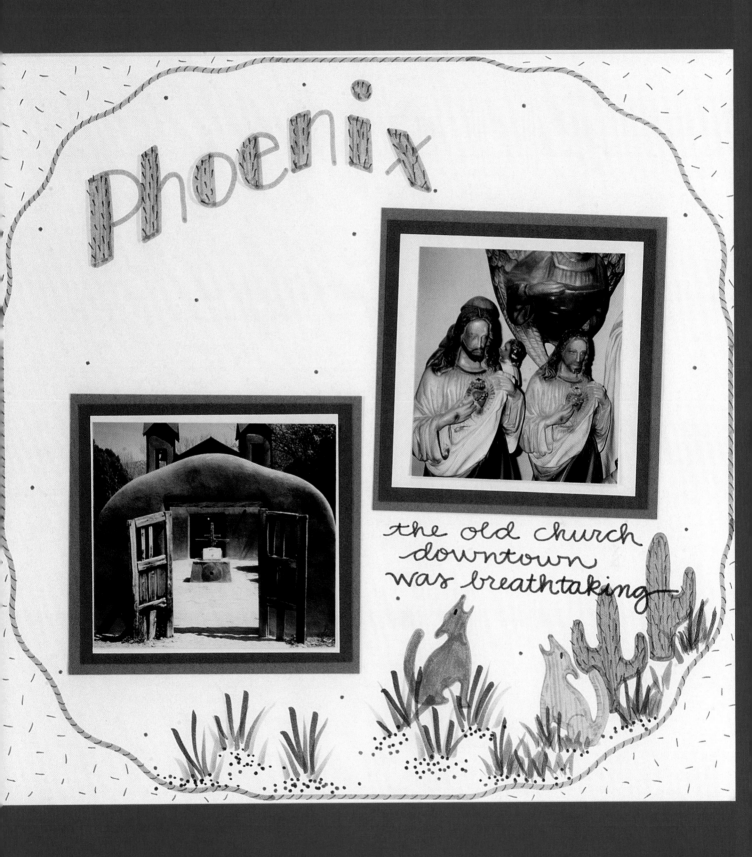

Phoenix: Wild West Round-It-Up, pens and paper. Trace the outside of the template. Add lines to make it look like a rope. Add the coyote icon. Draw in the grass.

...all · my

Flower Girls: Fall Round-It-Up. Flower Die Cut kit, paper, pen and scissors. Using the Fall template, trace the grass corners onto colored card stock. Cut them out and adhere the sides to the corners of the paper. Put a strip of paper inside the pockets. Tuck a few flowers here and there. Color in the centers. Add a schwoopie at the top of the photo.

i'm glad. i picked you all!

Field of Flowers

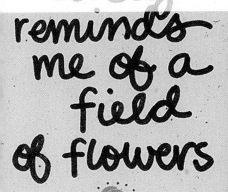

Field of Flowers: Buttons & Bows and Squiggles & Giggles Round-It-Up, Flower die cut, pens and paper. Draw a half circle using the Squiggles & Giggles Template. Fill the inside in, using all of the different flower icons. Fill the rest in with colored pens. Add the die cut using a pop-it-up foam dot.

reminds
me of a
field
of flowers

san francisco
1991

Title Pages: These were all done in the same way. Pick a Round-It-Up, Trace-It-Up, Dress-It-Up, a strip of paper, scissors and lots of pens! After you have laid out the title page color it in and cut it out. Add it to the top of your page.

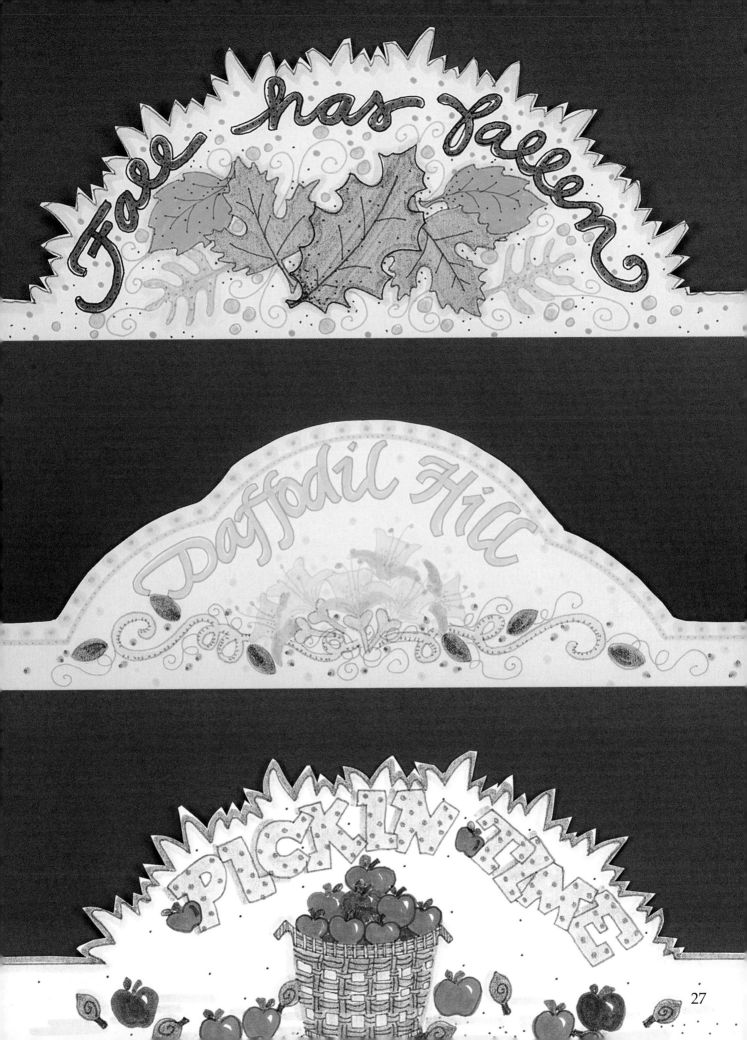

Fall has fallen

Daffodil Hill

PICKIN' TIME

BABY SHOWER

LULLABY

odnight... go to sleep little baby... close your eyes and good-nig

Cute
as a
Button

28

you and me and VICKEY Mouse

Vicky Mouse: Ahoy Matey, Deck The Halls Round-It-Up, Tam's Wacky Rule-It-Up, black card stock and scissors. Trace the outside of the template to trace the head. Use the inside to trace the ears. Cut the circles out and adhere them to the corner of your page. Use the bow in Deck The Halls, trace it on to red and white polka dot paper. Trace the top. Flip it over and trace it again. This makes the fluffy bow. Then adhere it onto the top of the head. Trace your circles and then add the lettering. Color and fill it in with detail.

Tom
Lindsay
&
Vickey
Mouse

· HIA 2000 ·

Carly got knighted as the Royal Queen

BIG TOP

Midevial Times

Hail to the Queen

Hail To The Queen Great Outdoors, Fall, Ahoy Matey Round-It-Up's, Zoo Die Cut Kit, paper, pens and Natural Cut Knife. Using the Great Outdoors trace the tent. Keep tracing pieces of the tent in different colors of paper and cut out. Adhere the strips on top of each other. Make a flag for the top using the Ahoy Matey. Trace the grass onto colored card stock and add the animals. Using Ahoy Matey add the stars and color it. This makes a great circus tent.

Summer Fun: Buttons & Bows Round-It-Up, Block-It-Up, Paper Corrugator by Paper Adventures. Trace the outside of the template to make the scoop. Make the cone rippled with the corrugator. Use the Block-It-Ups to do the lettering.

Girl Scouts

watermelon seed spitting
—c·o·n·t·e·s·t—

Girl Scouts Buttons & Bows. All Stars Round-It-Ups, paper, pens and scissors. Trace the watermelon circle onto colored card stock. Trace Ahoy Matey to make it look like a bite. Cut the zig zag out. Use the triangle shape to make the seeds.

1991

Shades of Carly: Squiggles & Giggles Round-It-Up, pen and paper. Using the inside of the template trace the five squares. Using the outside of the ruler trace the circle. Drop it down and trace it again. Using the fat end of a calligraphy pen, draw the checks between the lines. Use the icons to add the schwoopie look.

the flower children

at tom and vicky's wedding

The Flower Children: Buttons & Bows Round-It-Up, Natural Cut Knife, pens and paper. Trace the corners and cut out the circles leaving about an inch on each side. On a strip of white paper trace and color in the icons. Slip it into the pockets.

Bon
Appetit

Bob Appetit: Buttons & Bows, Squiggles & Giggles Round-It-Ups, White Milky Pen, acid-free doilies, pens and paper. Draw a square on your dark colored paper. Draw in the inside of the square with the white ink. Layer the flowers until the square is full.

when i Grow up ——...

Riley Jean: Buttons & Bows Round-It-Up, pens and paper. Trace the outside of the template to the bottom of your page. Drop it down and make a second line. Trace the flowers inside. Color them in.

Tap dancer or a ballerina or an artist... or maybe a kindergarten teacher. i'm not sure, yet!

...we've moved our Pad!

We Moved Our Pad: Squiggles & Giggles Round-It-Up, Flower Die Cut Kits, Frog from The Stamping Station 123's of Creative Doodling, scissors, paper and pens. Trace the outside of the template onto colored paper and cut it out. Adhere to the page and add the frog. Adhere the flowers with pop-it-up foam dots. Draw the doodles and frogs.

Spring: Deck the Halls, Fall, Squiggles & Giggles Round-It-Up, Cut-It-Up Die Cuts, Natural Cut Knife, paper and pens. Trace the outside of the template onto white paper. With the Squiggles & Giggles drop down and trace a line inside the circle. With the knife cut out the slots. Add the grass to the corner. Tuck a bunny leaping out of the circle. Add flowers on top of the grass. Use pop-it-up foam dots to give the flowers more dimension. Add a splash of color with random dots.

RUB ★ A ★ DUB

Bailey & Carly took a bath together...

Bailey decided to taste the soap... not a good idea!

BAILEY & CARLY IN A TUB

Disneyland Hotel

Rub A Dub: Baby Cakes Round-It-Up, pens and paper. Lay the Baby Cakes on the bottom of the page, trace it and move it over, trace it again. Add the ducks, but do not go below the lines. This gives it the appearance of floating on the surface. Add the circles to make it look like bubbles.

Jillian & Carly

Becoma

Sleepy: Baby Cakes Round-It-Up, Vicky's Tinkertoy upper and lower case Trace-It-Ups, paper and pens. Using the outside of the template trace the top and bottom of the page. This time use dots instead of a solid line. Add the icons and color them in.

sleepy

Flower Market: Ahoy Matey, All Star Round-It-Ups, Tam's Wacky Trace-It-Up, Natural Cut Knife, paper and pens. Trace the Circle from the Ahoy Matey. Then lay the All Star template under the circle and trace it. Cut the zig zag out and it now looks like a shopping bag. Trace the market letters onto a square piece of paper. Place them on top of the bag.

Pikes Market has the most amazing flower market. We were blooming with excitment.

42

SHIP AHOY

—Tom's New Toy—

Ship Ahoy: Ahoy Matey Round-It-Up, Bailey's Patches Trace-It-Up, Natural Cut Knife, paper and pens. Trace the corners of the paper with the Ahoy Matey template. Cut the top and bottom of the circle leaving about an inch on each side. You now have made corner pockets. Slip in some colored card stock and adhere your pictures. Trace each letter on a square then add to the top of the page.

on lake rollins

• Bachelor Party • 1999 •

Riley & McKenna

It's The Real Thing: Ahoy Matey, Squiggles and Giggles, Round-It-Ups, Flower Die Cut Kits, doilies, paper, pens and scissors. Trace the outside of the template. Lay the template inside the circle to make the smaller circles within the circle. Add the squares, triangles and circles inside the smaller circles. Color it all in. Use the inside of the template to cut the picture and put it into the center. Add the flowers to the outside. Cut the center of the doily out. Put the doily on top of the picture.

...it's the real thing

2000: Squiggles and Giggles Round-It-Up, Sailor white pen, scissors, paper and pens. Trace the Two onto card stock. Trace three circles onto the card stock. Using the inside of the template trace the squares and cut them out. Trace the photos and cut them into squares. Adhere the two and the three circles onto two pages. Affix the squares in the center at an angle. Next add the confetti and spirals with the white pen.

Trick or Treat: Ahoy Matey Round-It-Up, Halloween Rule-It-Up, Cut-It-Up ghost die cuts, Pop-It-Up foam dots, Lettering from the LMNOP Book, Me & My Big Ideas sticker strip, scissors, paper and pens. Using the Ahoy Matey template trace the circle onto a piece of card stock. Take the Halloween ruler to make the jagged edge. Cut them out to make it look like a treat sack. Add a piece of black paper to complete the bottom of the sack. Connect the two with the sticker. Add the ghosts to page with Pop-It-Up foam dots. Trick or Treat can be traced from the Lettering Book.

Boo To You: Great Outdoors Round-It-Up, Bailey's Patches Trace-It-Up, scissors, paper and pens. Trace the house and then cut it out. Add a crooked chimney, door and windows. Trace and cut out the grass. Adhere it to the front of the house. Do your lettering with Bailey's Patches. Outline the lettering to give it a shaded effect. Add the stars and cloud to finish off the design.

C H R I

Christmas

Our holiday tradition

'Twas the night before Christmas
with a dove in his hand
Santa spoke of goodwill
and peace through the land.

Christmas In The City: Deck The Halls Round-It-Up, Memories Forever Circle Punch, scissors,
Sailor white pen, paper and pens. Trace the outside of the template onto green card stock.
Cut it out and place it on top of the page matching the sides. Trace the Christmas lights,

in the city

saying farewell to I Magnin

"Twas the night before Christmas
and down on Montgomery.
Santa was checking his financial
summary. His cash flow was ebb
and that caused him to worry.
So off to his ATM machi
he did scurr

color them in and then add the lettering. Give it a snowy look by adding the white ink to the top of the letters. The Holly was traced and then cut out. The berries were punched out and added with Pop-It-Up foam dots. This is great for a two-page spread.

Holidaze: Deck The Halls Round-It-Up, Natural Cut Knife, Sailor white pen, paper and pens. Trace the outside of the template to the corners of the right hand side of the card stock. Leaving about an inch on each side cut the design out to form a pocket. Outline it with the white pen. Using a white strip of card stock trace the icons and color them in. Slip the strip into the pockets.

Jingle Bells: Deck The Halls Round-It-Up, Ahoy Matey Round-It-Ups, Tom's Casual Trace-It-Up, scissors, pens and paper. Trace the outside of the template for form a wreath. Trace the inside of the Ahoy Matey to form the center. Trace your photo and then cut it out. Adhere it to the center. Trace the top part of the page by tracing the outside of the template, move it, trace again and then cut out the page top. Add the lettering with Tom's Casual. Add a few icons and color them in also.

Camp Out: The Great Outdoors, Baby Cakes, Fall, Wild West Found-It-Ups. Bailey's Patches Trace-It-Up, Dress-It-Up rulers, scissors, paper and pens. Trace the outside of the tent on card stock and cut it out. Cut a slit up the front and fold the flap open. Trace the grass on the Fall template onto green card stock. Cut it out and put it in front of the tent. Trace the head onto a piece of card stock and add a t-shirt. Cut them out and slip them inside the tent. Using the moon and stars from the Baby Cakes template and the coyote from the Wild West, trace the letters and color them in to look like a plaid shirt.

Hangin' Out in New York: Dress-It-Up Rulers, Tam's Wacky, Memories Forever Paper Dolls, Renaissance Ribbon, Mini Clothes Pins, scissors, pens and paper. Trace the doll clothes onto white card stock. Cut them out and color them in. Hang them on to a ribbon clothes line with mini clothes pins. Make a sign using Tam's Wacky ruler. To make the envelope, take a paper doll, add hair and a face. Cut a square and adhere the doll to it. Cut all the pieces that hang off the square. The lettering is done with Tam's Wacky.

Wedding: Baby Cakes Round-It-Up, Dress-It-Up ruler. Make a pocket using the Baby Cakes template. Trace the top and then cut it out. Add the circle under the scallop to make it look like eyelet lace. Trace the dolls right on top of the pocket. The neat thing about using the doll templates is you can make them any way you want them. Add cards to the pocket and you have a great memorabilia page.

Little Cowpoke: Dress-It-Up ruler, Wild West Round-It-Up, Camping Block-It-Ups. Trace the doll, add the clothes and color them in. The cactus is added afterwards. Trace it so it looks like the cactus is behind him. This is a perfect spread for two pages. Just add icons from the template to tie the two pages together.

Paper Dolls: Dress-It-Ups, paper and pens. Trace the dolls, add the clothes and color them in to suit your picture needs.

56

Dress Up: Dress-It-Up ruler, Basics ruler, pens and paper. Use the square on the Basics Ruler using lines and dashes to trace the blocks. Overlap the squares and add lettering to them. Trace the clothes and color them in. Change the titles according to the pictures.

the gloves

the shoes

the shorts

the ears

the fun

disney brunch
and
a day at the park!

The Gloves: Dress-It-Up paper doll rulers, paper and pens. Trace the icons onto a square of white card stock. By using your imagination you can adapt the icons to match your photos. These were made to match photos that we had taken at Disneyland. This is a registered trademark of Buena Vista.